WITHDRAWN

5000241851

GW01280563

12/21

NORTH LINCOLNSHIRE COUNCIL

Library items can be renewed online 24/7, you will need your library card number and PIN.

Avoid library overdue charges by signing up to receive email preoverdue reminders at

http://www.opac.northlincs.gov.uk/

Follow us on Facebook
www.facebook.com/northlincolnshirelibraries

www.northlincs.gov.uk/libraries

Usborne
1000 English words

There's a useful word finder at the back of the book.

Listen to all the words at Usborne Quicklinks.

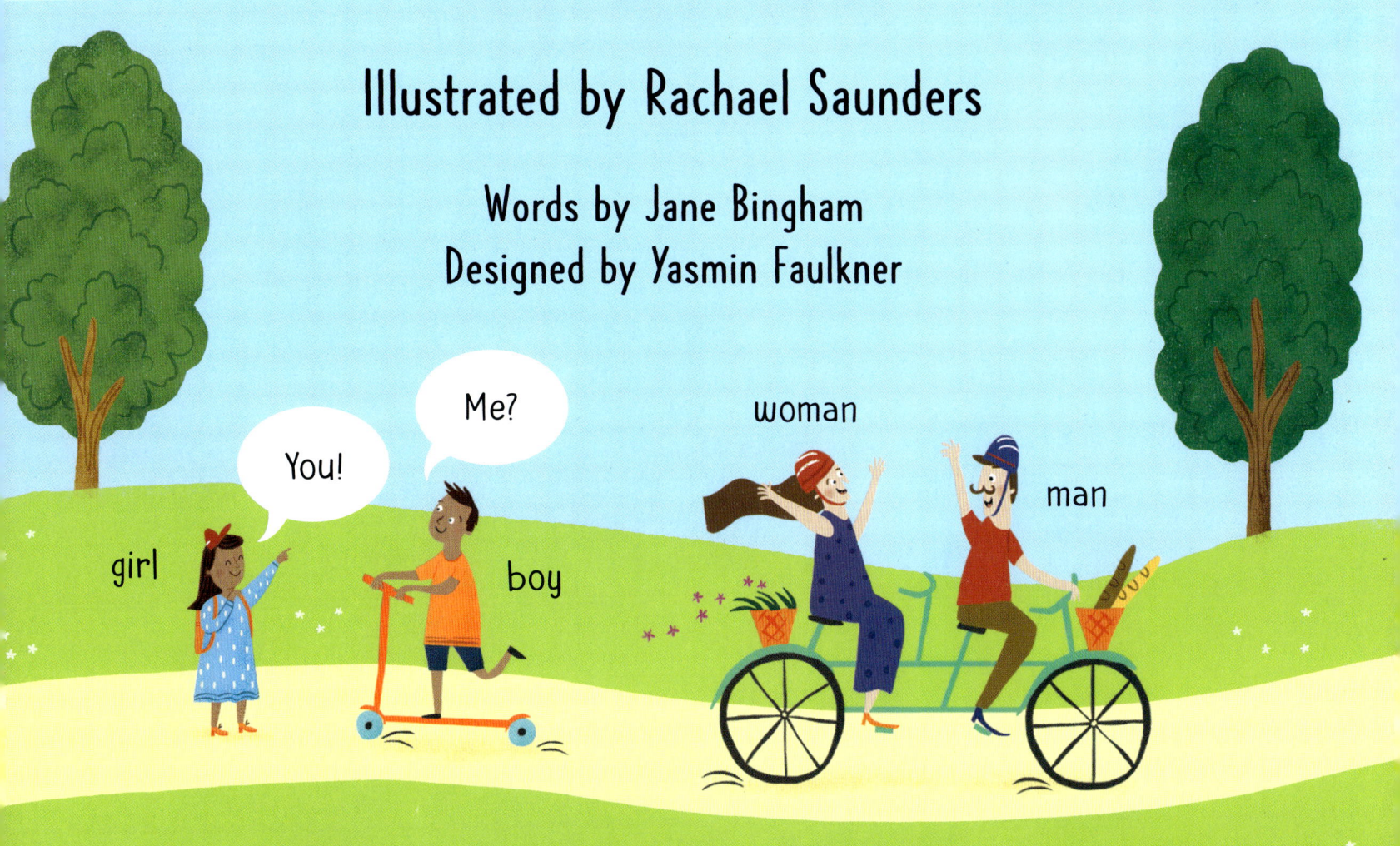

Illustrated by Rachael Saunders

Words by Jane Bingham
Designed by Yasmin Faulkner

You! Me? woman man
girl boy

Look out for QR codes like this throughout the book. You can scan each code to hear how to say the words or go to usborne.com/Quicklinks and type in the title of the book.

Contents

4 Home and family

6 In the kitchen

7 In the living room

8 Describing people

9 Clothes and things to wear

10 Your body

11 Your health

12 Food and drink

14 In the town

16 School words

17 All kinds of jobs

18 Sports words

19 Going out
20 Doing words  
22 Travel words 
24 In the countryside
25 At the seaside  
26 Around the world 
28 Weather and seasons
30 All kinds of animals  
32 Story words 
34 Opposites
35 Position words   
36 Days and numbers
37 Materials and amounts 
38 Colours, shapes and patterns

Home and family

Scan this code to hear how to say the words.

chimney

upstairs

downstairs

garage

poster
light
toy
game
floor

bedroom
ceiling
bathroom
bed
pillow
basin
toilet
carpet
duvet
sheet

living room
kitchen
television
sofa
sink
rug

inside
outside
stairs
wall
curtains
ladder
bag
bin
path
steps

suitcase
box

shower
tap
bath

clock
hob
counter

roof
shed

grandparents
grandpa grandma
grandfather grandmother

wife husband
mother father
mum dad
parents

daughter son
sister brother

uncle aunt
cousins

pet

grown-ups
children

buggy
garden baby twins

In the kitchen

pasta   rice   biscuits   cereal

jar   teapot   jug   cup

radio

shelf

microwave

jam   honey   can   bottle

saucepan   frying pan   salt   pepper

fridge

kettle

cupboard

cooking

cooker

dishwasher

bread   eggs   flour   sugar   bowl   recipe book

mixer

plug

Scan this code to hear how to say the words.

apron

stool

6

In the living room

fan

picture

door

blind

mirror

window

photo

plant

bookcase

radiator

Happy Birthday!

book

lamp

balloon

cake candle

magazine

comic

cushion

table

present

chair

card

birthday

newspaper

party

Scan this code to hear how to say the words.

Describing people

Scan this code to hear how to say the words.

happy angry excited sad surprised nervous scared brave

smile frown

kind upset sorry careful bored tired

shy friendly

funny

busy

naughty

thin fat short tall old young strong

Clothes and things to wear

Scan this code to hear how to say the words.

- t-shirt
- pyjamas
- dress
- ring
- zip
- jacket
- jeans
- skirt
- nightdress
- vest
- button
- pocket
- necklace
- sweater
- pants
- suit
- trousers
- socks
- slippers
- glasses
- tie
- watch
- belt
- shirt
- earrings
- tights
- shoes
- backpack
- bracelet
- sweatshirt
- handbag
- trainers

Your body

- hand
- head
- eye
- arm
- neck
- chest
- elbow
- bottom
- knee
- leg
- eyebrow
- ear
- nose
- thumb
- shoulder
- fingers
- stomach
- back
- toes
- foot

Scan this code to hear how to say the words.

- hair
- straight
- curly
- wash
- sponge
- teeth
- mouth
- face
- toothpaste
- toothbrush
- hairbrush
- comb
- shampoo
- soap

Your health

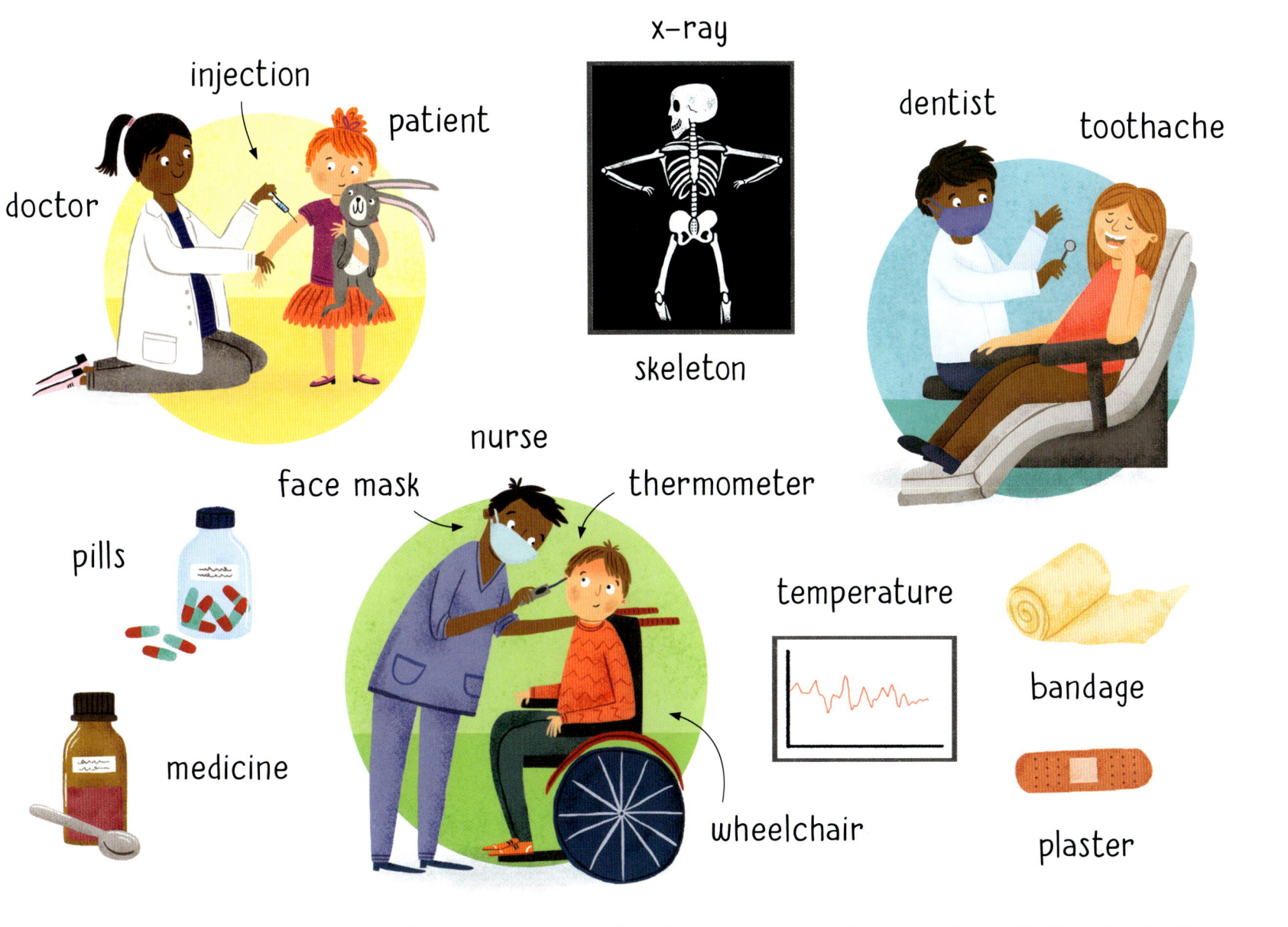

Scan this code to hear how to say the words.

injection

doctor

patient

x-ray

skeleton

dentist

toothache

pills

medicine

face mask

nurse

thermometer

temperature

wheelchair

bandage

plaster

hand sanitiser

tissue

sneeze

cold

cough

headache

stomachache

earache

food and drink

Scan this code to hear how to say the words.

vegetables

- cucumber
- carrot
- onion
- cabbage
- potatoes
- aubergine
- beans
- chillies
- peas
- mushrooms

drinks

- water
- coffee
- juice
- tea

dairy

- cream
- cheese
- butter
- yogurt
- milk

curry

chocolate

burger

pizza

sandwich

soup

nuts

fruit

melon
grapes
strawberries
raspberries
apple
pear
pineapple
lemon
banana
mango
orange

meat and fish

chicken
salmon
prawns
tuna
sausage
steak

salad
lettuce
tomato
chopsticks
noodles
chips
taste
crisps
sweets
love
hate

In the town

- playground
- swings
- slide
- swimming pool
- skyscraper
- park
- library
- flowerbed
- statue
- school
- factory
- chemist
- sports centre
- bank
- theatre
- police station
- hospital
- supermarket
- airport
- car park
- runway

Scan this code to hear how to say the words.

- temple
- office
- market
- lift
- flats
- stadium
- post office
- hairdresser
- shops
- mosque
- fire station
- shopping centre
- church
- museum
- synagogue
- restaurant
- cinema
- snack bar
- digger
- crane
- road

School words

class
classroom
alphabet

a b c d e f g h i j k l m n o p q r s t u v w x y z

lessons
- art
- science
- history
- geography
- music
- spelling
- maths
- reading
- writing

peg · name

board · teacher
apple — letter
bat — word

computer
screen · mouse
keyboard · desk

write · workbook · read
pen · ruler

scissors · glue
cut · make · sing

draw · paint
drawing · painting
pencil
rubber
song

Scan this code to hear how to say the words.

All kinds of jobs

Scan this code to hear how to say the words.

writer

designer

artist

photographer — camera

ballerina

mechanic

vet

scientist

footballer

gardener

chef

carpenter

builder

businessman   businesswoman

reporter

actor

police officer — badge

lawyer

soldier

uniform — firefighter

17

Sports words

Scan this code to hear how to say the words.

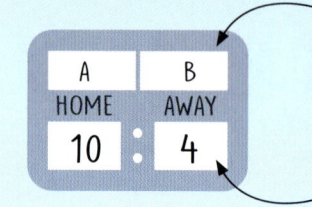

team — score

A HOME	B AWAY
10	4

bat — racket — hit — football

baseball · tennis · badminton · referee · kick

ball

race · win · volleyball · basketball · gymnastics

push · pull · jump · spin · turn

bicycle · helmet · prize

cycling · hiking · riding · skateboarding · snowboarding · skiing

18

Going out

Scan this code to hear how to say the words.

Café

- menu
- waiter
- customer
- bill
- pay
- money
- plate
- tray
- sauce
- fork
- knife
- hungry
- eat
- spoon
- thirsty
- drink
- glass

meals
- breakfast
- lunch
- tea
- dinner

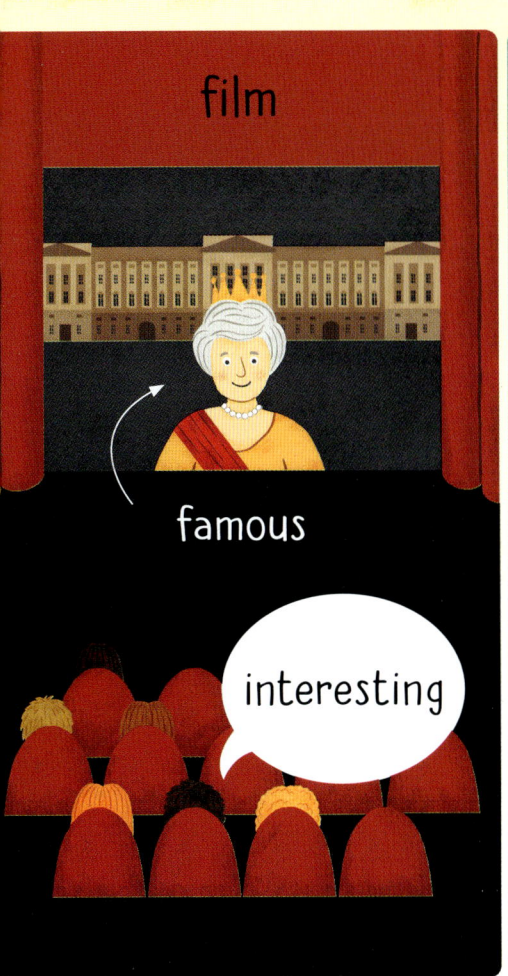

film
- famous
- interesting

concert
- piano
- drums
- band
- guitar
- singer
- dancing
- fun

circus
- clown
- acrobat
- exciting

19

Doing words

whisper laugh

friends

climb

think

fly

find

stand

point hide

watch

see

sit

lie down

hear

HELLO!

shout

wave

meet

run

Hi!

smell

talk

walk

Scan this code to hear how to say the words.

choose	buy	sell	give	take

sleep — holiday — wake up — dream

lend — borrow

phoning — mobile — texting — headset — computer game
tablet — typing — laptop — listen — look — play

pick up — carry — drop — cry — help
trip — fall — break — mend

21

Travel words

plane

car

bus

wait

bus stop

driver

taxi

motorbike

stop

traffic lights

Scan this code to hear how to say the words.

petrol station

accident

windscreen

engine

sail

wheel

boat

yacht

canoe

pilot　　helicopter　　hot-air balloon

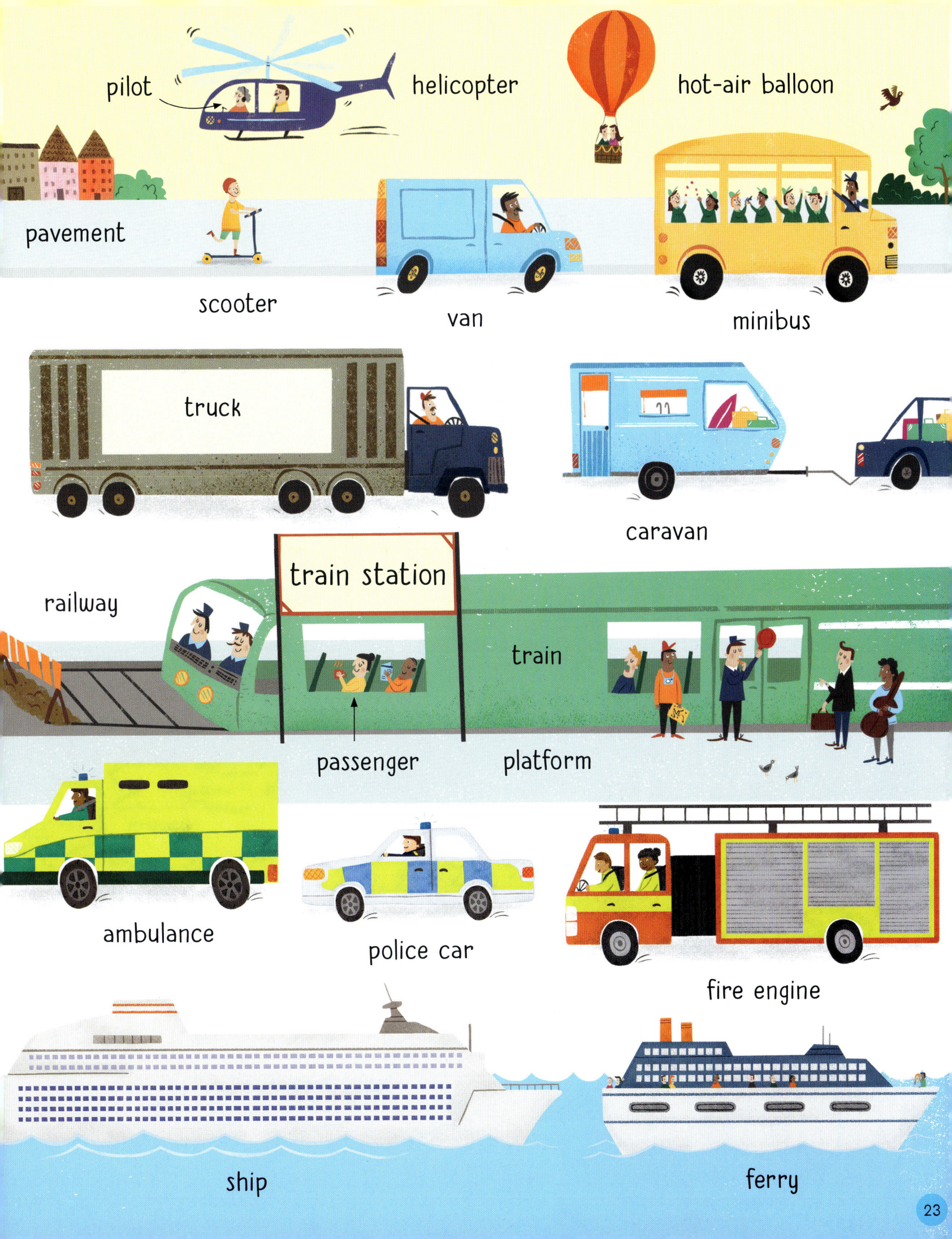

pavement

scooter　　van　　minibus

truck　　caravan

railway　　train station　　train

passenger　　platform

ambulance　　police car　　fire engine

ship　　ferry

In the countryside

Scan this code to hear how to say the words.

- hill
- field
- valley
- village
- barn
- river
- farm
- farmer
- bush
- house
- hay
- tree
- tractor
- bird
- nest
- gate
- grass
- fence
- butterfly
- bridge
- stream
- wasp
- fly
- insects
- bee
- caterpillar
- leaf
- snail
- flower
- squirrel

24

At the seaside

- seagull
- hotel
- ice cream
- tent
- cliff
- hut
- lifeguard
- cave
- harbour
- sea
- fishing net
- throw
- catch
- sand
- towel
- spade
- beach
- bucket
- sandcastle
- wave
- swimsuit
- surfboard
- swim

Scan this code to hear how to say the words.

Around the world

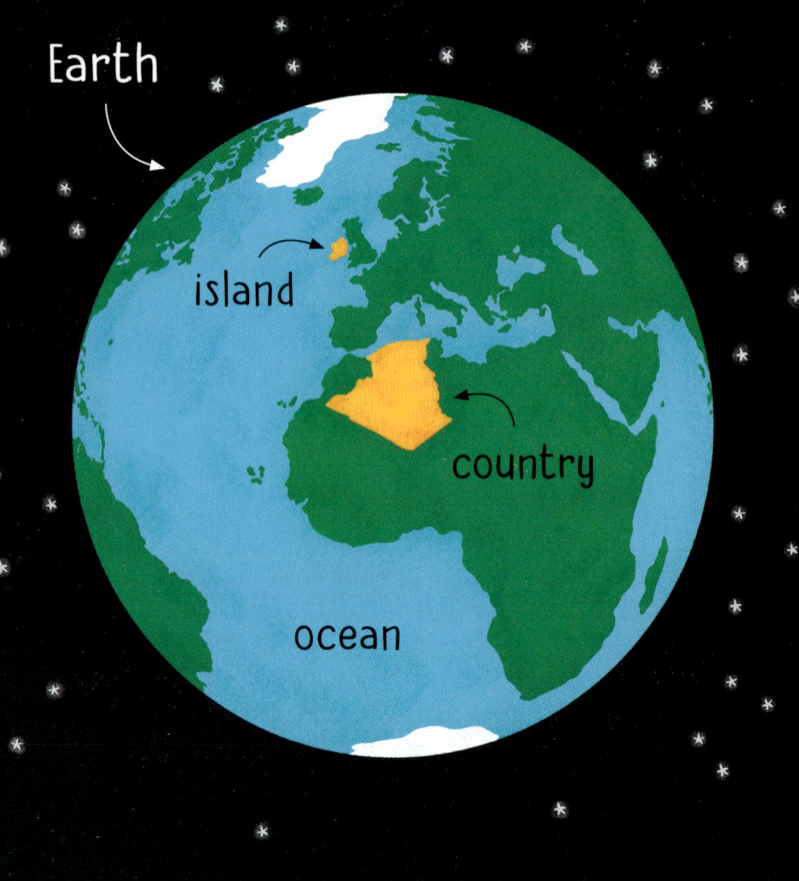

Earth
island
country
ocean

desert
sand dune
camel
oasis
palm tree

city
street

jungle
snake
monkey
leopard
parrot

Scan this code to hear how to say the words.

- waterfall
- mountain
- forest
- bear
- lake
- fish
- jellyfish
- seaweed
- diver
- octopus
- starfish
- turtle
- rock
- shell
- crab
- penguin
- iceberg
- seal
- whale

Weather and seasons

Scan this code to hear how to say the words.

sky

rainbow

sun

cloud

hot

rain

wet

puddle

umbrella

basket picnic

cap

sunglasses

boots dry

suncream

shorts

raincoat

mud

sandals

pond

28

snowflake

snow

cold

icicle

snowman
warm
hat
coat
snowball
gloves
scarf
ice-skating
ice

spring   summer

seasons

winter   autumn

thunder lightning   frosty

stormy

windy
kite
misty

torch

29

All kinds of animals

Scan this code to hear how to say the words.

tiger

gorilla

lion — mane

kangaroo

horn   rhino

wolf

trunk

elephant

giraffe

fur

panda

tail   zebra

ZOO

crocodile

hippo   dolphin   shark

wing — eagle — beak

fox

deer

horse

pony

bull

cow

swan

goat

sheep

lamb

donkey

duck

cockerel

rabbit

dog

mouse

rat

cat

kittens

puppies

chicks

hen

31

Story words

Scan this code to hear how to say the words.

palace — crown — princess — prince — king — queen — carriage

knight — sword — shield — flag — castle — wand — dragon — frog

wood — fairy — elf

wizard — magic — witch — giant — beard

moon
owl
ghost
bat

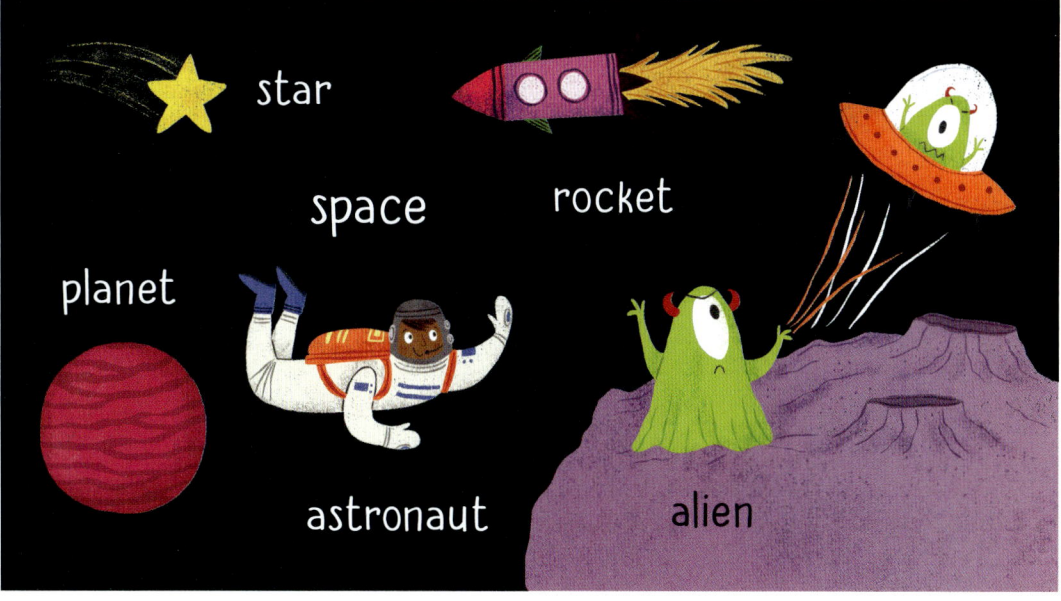

star
space
planet
rocket
astronaut
alien

desert island
pirate
mermaid
treasure
beautiful

monster fierce

envelope stamp letter
address key

spider
explorer
web
map
lizard

inventor robot
clever

Opposites

Scan this code to hear how to say the words.

open — closed

same — different

slow — fast

difficult — easy

clean — dirty

heavy — light

noisy — quiet

old — new

hard — soft

back — front

light — dark

wrong — right

good — better — best

bad — worse — worst

Position words

Scan this code to hear how to say the words.

left   next to   right

up

far

above

below

down

near   here

there

in front of   between   behind

on   off

into   out of

from   to   around   across   opposite

over   through   under   in   out   away

Days and numbers

Scan this code to hear how to say the words.

days of the week

- Monday
- Tuesday
- Wednesday
- Thursday
- Friday

weekend

- Saturday
- Sunday

morning 07:00

afternoon 16:00

evening 19:00

night 23:00

0	zero		
1	one	11	eleven
2	two	12	twelve
3	three	13	thirteen
4	four	14	fourteen
5	five	15	fifteen
6	six	16	sixteen
7	seven	17	seventeen
8	eight	18	eighteen
9	nine	19	nineteen
10	ten	20	twenty

date → 12th
month → FEBRUARY
year → 2025

diary

Dear diary, today I....

next   last

first   second   third

Materials and amounts

Scan this code to hear how to say the words.

cotton   glass   wood   stone

wool   metal   plastic   rubber

top
corner
centre
paper
bottom

full   empty   subtract   add

big
little
small
large

whole   half   quarter   short   long

missing

few   fewer   fewest   many   more   most

Colours, shapes and patterns

Scan this code to hear how to say the words.

red
orange
yellow
pink
purple
green
brown
blue
black
white
grey
silver
gold

square
triangle
rectangle
star
round
circle

lines
spots
stripes

A-Z WORD FINDER

Do you need to find a particular word? All 1000 words in this book are listed here.

A

above 35
accident 22
acrobat 19
across 35
actor 17
add 37
address 33
afternoon 36
airport 14
alien 33
alphabet 16
ambulance 23
amounts 37
angry 8
animals 30
apple 13
apron 6
arm 10
around 35
art 16
artist 17
astronaut 33
aubergine 12
aunt 5
autumn 29
away 35

B

baby 5
back (body) 10
back (not front) 34

backpack 9
bad 34
badge 17
badminton 18
bag 4
ball 18
ballerina 17
balloon 7
banana 13
band 19
bandage 11
bank 14
barn 24
baseball 18
basin 4
basket 28
basketball 18
bat 18
bat (animal) 33
bath 5
bathroom 4
beach 25
beak 31
beans 12
bear 27
beard 32
beautiful 33
bed 4
bedroom 4
bee 24
behind 35
below 35

belt 9
best 34
better 34
between 35
bicycle 18
big 37
bill 19
bin 4
bird 24
birthday 7
biscuits 6
black 38
blind 7
blue 38
board 16
boat 22
body 10
book 7
bookcase 7
boots 28
bored 8
borrow 21
bottle 6
bottom (body) 10
bottom 37
bowl 6
box 5
boy 1
bracelet 9
brave 8
bread 6
break 21

You can also listen to all the words at Usborne Quicklinks.
Go to usborne.com/Quicklinks and type in 1000 English Words.

breakfast 19
bridge 24
brother 5
brown 38
bucket 25
buggy 5
builder 17
bull 31
burger 12
bus 22
bus stop 22
bush 24
businessman 17
businesswoman 17
busy 8
butter 12
butterfly 24
button 9
buy 21

C

cabbage 12
café 19
cake 7
camel 26
camera 17
can 6
candle 7
canoe 22
cap 28
car 22
car park 14
caravan 23
card 7
careful 8
carpenter 17

carpet 4
carriage 32
carrot 12
carry 21
castle 32
cat 31
catch 25
caterpillar 24
cave 25
ceiling 4
centre 37
cereal 6
chair 7
cheese 12
chef 17
chemist 14
chest 10
chicken 13
chicks 31
children 5
chillies 12
chimney 4
chips 13
chocolate 12
choose 21
chopsticks 13
church 15
cinema 15
circle 38
circus 19
city 26
class 16
classroom 16
clean 34
clever 33
cliff 25

climb 20
clock 5
closed 34
clothes 9
cloud 28
clown 19
coat 29
cockerel 31
coffee 12
cold (illness) 11
cold 29
colours 38
comb 10
comic 7
computer 16
computer game 21
concert 19
cooker 6
cooking 6
corner 37
cotton 37
cough 11
counter 5
country 26
countryside 24
cousins 5
cow 31
crab 27
crane 15
cream 12
crisps 13
crocodile 30
crown 32
cry 21
cucumber 12
cup 6

cupboard 6
curly 10
curry 12
curtains 4
cushion 7
customer 19
cut 16
cycling 18

D
dad 5
dairy 12
dancing 19
dark 34
date 36
daughter 5
days 36
deer 31
dentist 11
desert 26
desert island 33
designer 17
desk 16
diary 36
different 34
difficult 34
digger 15
dinner 19
dirty 34
dishwasher 6
diver 27
doctor 11
dog 31
dolphin 30
donkey 31
door 7

down 35
downstairs 4
dragon 32
draw 16
drawing 16
dream 21
dress 9
drink (to drink) 19
drinks 12
driver 22
drop 21
drums 19
dry 28
duck 31
duvet 4

E
eagle 31
ear 10
earache 11
earrings 9
Earth 26
easy 34
eat 19
eggs 6
eight 36
eighteen 36
elbow 10
elephant 30
eleven 36
elf 32
empty 37
engine 22
envelope 33
evening 36
excited 8

exciting 19
explorer 33
eye 10
eyebrow 10

F
face 10
face mask 11
factory 14
fairy 32
fall 21
family 4
famous 19
fan 7
far 35
farm 24
farmer 24
fast 34
fat 8
father 5
fence 24
ferry 23
few 37
fewer 37
fewest 37
field 24
fierce 33
fifteen 36
film 19
find 20
fingers 10
fire engine 23
fire station 15
firefighter 17
first 36
fish (food) 13

fish 27
fishing net 25
five 36
flag 32
flats 15
floor 4
flour 6
flower 24
flowerbed 14
fly (to fly) 20
fly (insect) 24
food 12
foot 10
football 18
footballer 17
forest 27
fork 19
four 36
fourteen 36
fox 31
Friday 36
fridge 6
friendly 8
friends 20
frog 32
from 35
front 34
frosty 29
frown 8
fruit 13
frying pan 6
full 37
fun 19
funny 8
fur 30

G

game 4
garage 4
garden 5
gardener 17
gate 24
geography 16
ghost 33
giant 32
giraffe 30
girl 1
give 21
glass 19
glass (material) 37
glasses 9
gloves 29
glue 16
goat 31
gold 38
good 34
gorilla 30
grandfather 5
grandma 5
grandmother 5
grandpa 5
grandparents 5
grapes 13
grass 24
green 38
grey 38
grown-ups 5
guitar 19
gymnastics 18

H

hair 10
hairbrush 10
hairdresser 15
half 37
hand 10
hand sanitiser 11
handbag 9
happy 8
harbour 25
hard (not soft) 34
hat 29
hate 13
hay 24
head 10
headache 11
headset 21
health 11
hear 20
heavy 34
helicopter 23
hello 20
helmet 18
help 21
hen 31
here 35
hi 20
hide 20
hiking 18
hill 24
hippo 30
history 16
hit 18
hob 5
holiday 21

home 4
honey 6
horn 30
horse 31
hospital 14
hot 28
hot-air balloon 23
hotel 25
house 24
hungry 19
husband 5
hut 25

I
ice 29
ice cream 25
ice-skating 29
iceberg 27
icicle 29
in 35
in front of 35
injection 11
insects 24
inside 4
interesting 19
into 35
inventor 33
island 26

J
jacket 9
jam 6
jar 6
jeans 9
jellyfish 27
jobs 17

jug 6
juice 12
jump 18
jungle 26

K
kangaroo 30
kettle 6
key 33
keyboard 16
kick 18
kind 8
king 32
kitchen 4, 6
kite 29
kittens 31
knee 10
knife 19
knight 32

L
ladder 4
lake 27
lamb 31
lamp 7
laptop 21
large 37
last 36
laugh 20
lawyer 17
leaf 24
left 35
leg 10
lemon 13
lend 21
leopard 26

lessons 16
letter (alphabet) 16
letter 33
lettuce 13
library 14
lie down 20
lifeguard 25
lift (in building) 15
light (electric) 4
light (not dark) 34
light (not heavy) 34
lightning 29
lines 38
lion 30
listen 21
little 37
living room 4, 7
lizard 33
long 37
look 21
love 13
lunch 19

M
magazine 7
magic 32
make 16
man 1
mane 30
mango 13
many 37
map 33
market 15
materials 37
maths 16
me 1

meals 19
meat 13
mechanic 17
medicine 11
meet 20
melon 13
mend 21
menu 19
mermaid 33
metal 37
microwave 6
milk 12
minibus 23
mirror 7
missing 37
misty 29
mixer 6
mobile 21
Monday 36
money 19
monkey 26
monster 33
month 36
moon 33
more 37
morning 36
mosque 15
most 37
mother 5
motorbike 22
mountain 27
mouse (computer) 16
mouse 31
mouth 10
mud 28
mum 5

museum 15
mushrooms 12
music 16

N

name 16
naughty 8
near 35
neck 10
necklace 9
nervous 8
nest 24
new 34
newspaper 7
next 36
next to 35
night 36
nightdress 9
nine 36
nineteen 36
noisy 34
noodles 13
nose 10
numbers 36
nurse 11
nuts 12

O

oasis 26
ocean 26
octopus 27
off 35
office 15
old 8, 34
on 35
one 36

onion 12
open 34
opposite (not the same) 34
opposite (position) 35
orange (fruit) 13
orange 38
out 35
out of 35
outside 4
over 35
owl 33

P

paint 16
painting 16
palace 32
palm tree 26
panda 30
pants 9
paper 37
parents 5
park 14
parrot 26
party 7
passenger 23
pasta 6
path 4
patient 11
patterns 38
pavement 23
pay 19
pear 13
peas 12
peg 16
pen 16
pencil 16

penguin 27
people 8
pepper 6
pet 5
petrol station 22
phoning 21
photo 7
photographer 17
piano 19
pick up 21
picnic 28
picture 7
pillow 4
pills 11
pilot 23
pineapple 13
pink 38
pirate 33
pizza 12
plane 22
planet 33
plant 7
plaster 11
plastic 37
plate 19
platform 23
play (to play) 21
playground 14
plug 6
pocket 9
point 20
police car 23
police officer 17
police station 14
pond 28
pony 31

position 35
post office 15
poster 4
potatoes 12
prawns 13
present 7
prince 32
princess 32
prize 18
puddle 28
pull 18
puppies 31
purple 38
push 18
pyjamas 9

Q
quarter 37
queen 32
quiet 34

R
rabbit 31
race 18
racket 18
radiator 7
radio 6
railway 23
rain 28
rainbow 28
raincoat 28
raspberries 13
rat 31
read 16
reading 16
recipe book 6

rectangle 38
red 38
referee 18
reporter 17
restaurant 15
rhino 30
rice 6
riding 18
right (correct) 34
right (not left) 35
ring (jewellery) 9
river 24
road 15
robot 33
rock 27
rocket 33
roof 5
round (shape) 38
rubber 16
rubber (material) 37
rug 4
ruler 16
run 20
runway 14

S
sad 8
sail 22
salad 13
salmon 13
salt 6
same 34
sand 25
sand dune 26
sandals 28
sandcastle 25

sandwich 12
Saturday 36
sauce 19
saucepan 6
sausage 13
scared 8
scarf 29
school 14, 16
science 16
scientist 17
scissors 16
scooter 23
score 18
screen 16
sea 25
seagull 25
seal 27
seaside 25
seasons 29
seaweed 27
second 36
see 20
sell 21
seven 36
seventeen 36
shampoo 10
shapes 38
shark 30
shed 5
sheep 31
sheet 4
shelf 6
shell 27
shield 32
ship 23
shirt 9

shoes 9
shopping centre 15
shops 15
short (person) 8
short 37
shorts 28
shoulder 10
shout 20
shower 5
shy 8
silver 38
sing 16
singer 19
sink 4
sister 5
sit 20
six 36
sixteen 36
skateboarding 18
skeleton 11
skiing 18
skirt 9
sky 28
skyscraper 14
sleep 21
slide 14
slippers 9
slow 34
small 37
smell 20
smile 8
snack bar 15
snail 24
snake 26
sneeze 11
snow 29

snowball 29
snowboarding 18
snowflake 29
snowman 29
soap 10
socks 9
sofa 4
soft 34
soldier 17
son 5
song 16
sorry 8
soup 12
space 33
spade 25
spelling 16
spider 33
spin 18
sponge 10
spoon 19
sports 18
sports centre 14
spots 38
spring (season) 29
square 38
squirrel 24
stadium 15
stairs 4
stamp 33
stand 20
star 33
star (shape) 38
starfish 27
statue 14
steak 13
steps 4

stomach 10
stomachache 11
stone 37
stool 6
stop 22
stormy 29
story 32
straight 10
strawberries 13
stream 24
street 26
stripes 38
strong 8
subtract 37
sugar 6
suit 9
suitcase 5
summer 29
sun 28
suncream 28
Sunday 36
sunglasses 28
supermarket 14
surfboard 25
surprised 8
swan 31
sweater 9
sweatshirt 9
sweets 13
swim 25
swimming pool 14
swimsuit 25
swings 14
sword 32
synagogue 15

T

table 7
tablet 21
tail 30
take 21
talk 20
tall 8
tap 5
taste 13
taxi 22
tea 12
tea (meal) 19
teacher 16
team 18
teapot 6
teeth 10
television 4
temperature 11
temple 15
ten 36
tennis 18
tent 25
texting 21
theatre 14
there 35
thermometer 11
thin 8
think 20
third 36
thirsty 19
thirteen 36
three 36
through 35
throw 25
thumb 10

thunder 29
Thursday 36
tie 9
tiger 30
tights 9
tired 8
tissue 11
to 35
toes 10
toilet 4
tomato 13
toothache 11
toothbrush 10
toothpaste 10
top 37
torch 29
towel 25
town 14
toy 4
tractor 24
traffic lights 22
train 23
train station 23
trainers 9
travel 22
tray 19
treasure 33
tree 24
triangle 38
trip (to trip) 21
trousers 9
truck 23
trunk (elephant) 30
t-shirt 9
Tuesday 36
tuna 13

turn 18
turtle 27
twelve 36
twenty 36
twins 5
two 36
typing 21

U
umbrella 28
uncle 5
under 35
uniform 17
up 35
upset 8
upstairs 4

V
valley 24
van 23
vegetables 12
vest 9
vet 17
village 24
volleyball 18

W
wait 22
waiter 19
wake up 21
walk 20
wall 4
wand 32
warm 29
wash 10
wasp 24

watch 9
watch (to watch) 20
water 12
waterfall 27
wave (to wave) 20
wave 25
wear 9
weather 28
web 33
Wednesday 36
week 36
weekend 36
wet 28
whale 27
wheel 22
wheelchair 11
whisper 20
white 38
whole 37
wife 5
win 18
window 7
windscreen 22
windy 29
wing 31
winter 29
witch 32
wizard 32
wolf 30
woman 1
wood 32
wood (material) 37
wool 37
word 16
workbook 16
world 26

worse 34
worst 34
write 16
writer 17
writing 16
wrong 34

X
x-ray 11

Y
yacht 22
year 36
yellow 38
yogurt 12
you 1
young 8

Z
zebra 30
zero 36
zip 9
zoo 30